MOTHER GOOSE

ITSY BITSY SPIDER

And Other Clap-Along Rhymes

Illustrated by
Sanja Rescek, Elke Zins-Meister, Eric Smith,
Katy Taggart and Jacqueline East

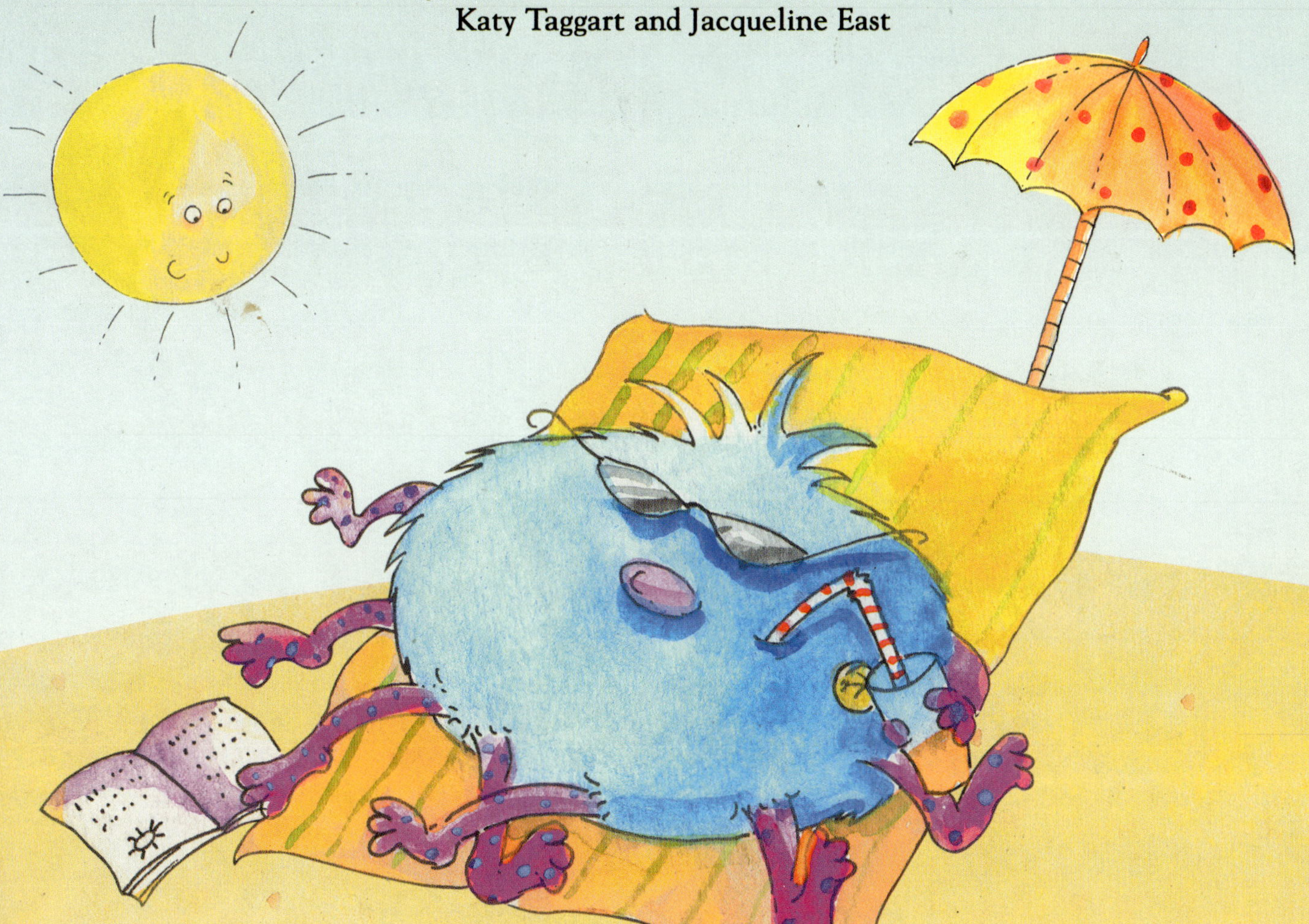

CLAP-ALONGS

Itsy Bitsy Spider

The itsy bitsy spider
climbed up
the water spout

Down came the rain

And washed
the spider out

Out came the sun

And dried up
all the rain

And the itsy bitsy spider
climbed up
the spout again

Here Is the Church

Here is the church

Here is the steeple

Open the doors

And see all the people

Where Is Thumbkin?

Where is thumbkin?
Where is thumbkin?

Here I am.

Here I am.

How are you today, sir?
Very well, I thank you.

Run away.

Run away.

Where is pointer?
Where is pointer?

Here I am.

Here I am.

How are you today, sir?
Very well, I thank you.

Run away.

Run away.

BINGO

There was a farmer had a dog
And Bingo was his name-o

B-i-n-g-o, B-i-n-g-o, B-i-n-g-o
And Bingo was his name-o

There was a farmer had a dog

And Bingo was his name-o

(clap)-i-n-g-o
(clap)-i-n-g-o
(clap)-i-n-g-o

And Bingo was his name-o

There was a farmer had a dog

And Bingo was his name-o

(clap)-(clap)-n-g-o
(clap)-(clap)-n-g-o
(clap)-(clap)-n-g-o

And Bingo was his name-o

There was a farmer had a dog
And Bingo was his name-o

(clap)-(clap)-(clap)-g-o
(clap)-(clap)-(clap)-g-o
(clap)-(clap)-(clap)-g-o

And Bingo was his name-o

There was a farmer had a dog
And Bingo was his name-o

(clap)-(clap)-(clap)-(clap)-o
(clap)-(clap)-(clap)-(clap)-o
(clap)-(clap)-(clap)-(clap)-o

And Bingo was his name-o

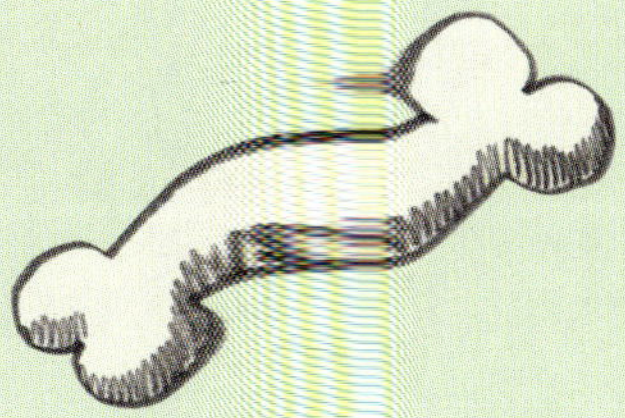

There was a farmer had a dog
And Bingo was his name-o

(clap)-(clap)-(clap)-(clap)-(clap)
(clap)-(clap)-(clap)-(clap)-(clap)
(clap)-(clap)-(clap)-(clap)-(clap)

And Bingo was his name-o

Pat-a-Cake

Pat-a-cake, pat-a-cake

baker's man

Bake me a cake

As fast as you can

Roll it and prick it

And mark it with a "B"